WORLD'S WORST
TRAVEL DESTINATIONS

DOG 'n' BONE

WORLD'S WORST
TRAVEL DESTINATIONS

50 travel experiences
you will want
to miss...

DOG 'n' BONE

Published in 2012 by Dog 'n' Bone Books
An imprint of Ryland Peters & Small Ltd.
20–21 Jockey's Fields   519 Broadway, 5th Floor
London WC1R 4BW   New York, NY 10012

www.dogandbonebooks.com

10 9 8 7 6 5 4 3 2 1

A CIP catalog record for this book is available from the Library of
Congress and the British Library.

ISBN: 978 0 957140 92 9

Printed in China

Editor: Tim Leng
Designer: Wide Open Design
See page 128 for picture credits

For digital editions, visit www.cicobooks.com/apps.php

CONTENTS

INTRODUCTION

Is there anything more annoying than listening to someone's holiday stories? Sorry, it wasn't a holiday; it was "traveling." You didn't go away simply to lie in the sun and read a celebrity autobiography, guzzle the local booze, avoid getting sunburnt as much as possible, and embrace the culture by taking a trip to a market to buy some malformed wooden ornaments—you embarked on a mission to unlock new experiences that would help you grow as a person.

How many times have you witnessed people coming over all glassy eyed as they've earnestly explained how seeing people living in poverty has helped them realize we don't need amenities like supermarkets and games consoles?

For me, it was one time too many, which is what inspired me to write this book.

There's a fine line between a must-see destination and a no-go zone, and quite often what makes one place such an enlightening haven is what makes another a terrifying no no.

Strange cuisine, eager locals, historic customs, environmental anomalies, and fellow holiday makers are just some of the criteria that can make the difference between a trip to paradise and a holiday from hell.

Foodies may flock to France to feast on foie gras and savor every mouthful of a freshly baked, flaky croissant, but in Taiwan one of the most popular places to dine is the Modern Toilet chain of restaurants, where you can eat a bubbling chicken curry direct from the bowl of a porcelain throne.

Sickening snacks are also the norm in Cambodia, where you can enjoy a snake on a skewer or a deep-fried tarantula. Just be careful not to eat the abdomen—it might ooze what looks like the inside of a Kinder Bueno, but it's actually a gloop of feces, eggs, and innards.

The inhabitants of the Florida city of Celebration, meanwhile, were attracted by its ethos of a "return to small town values." Based on the ideals of Walt Disney, locals love to smile and really get to know their neighbors. Visitors who have roamed the streets of saccharine houses whisper that it has more than a slight air of Stepford Wives about it, however.

Elsewhere, thousands of people flock to see the Northern Lights every year—yet fewer people seem as keen to spend even one night in the Mongolian city of Ulan Bator, the world's most remote capital city which enjoys a near-subarctic climate.

And spare a thought for people who take a summer trip to Cave-in-Rock in Illinois. For one week each year, it is overrun with whooping Insane Clown Posse fans who meet up to party, listen to rap music, and watch wrestling as part of the Gathering of the Juggalos festival. Similarly, the beautiful Greek island of Corfu used to be the holiday destination of choice for Europe's royals before it became a package holiday hotspot. Now the

streets of its largest town, Kavos, are a minefield of vomit, crying teenagers, and discarded condoms.

Perhaps after reading this book, you will agree with me that terrible, dangerous, depraved, ungodly places are the best ones to visit. If only because the stories you'll be telling weeks, months, even years later are sure to be a lot more entertaining than describing an "amazing waterfall" that anyone can experience by simply looking it up on the Internet.

Kara Simsek

• North Pole, AK

Manchester, England

Breda,
Hollan•

Egremont Crab Fair, England •

• Vulcan, Canada

Cleveland, OH

Anthrocon, Pittsburgh, PA

Dalby, Isle of Man•
Pluckley, England•

Bugarach, France
Lekeitio, Spain

Hell, MI •

• Weir's Beach, NH

Evansville, IN •
Cave-In-Rock, IL

Boring, MD

•Jersey Shore, NJ

Beebe, AR •

• East Dublin, GA

Celebration, FL •

• Bermuda Triangle

• Haiti

Benin •

Festac Town, Nigeria •

• Nuku Hiva, French Polynesia

• Pitcairn Island

Tristan da Cunha •

• Norilsk, Russia

• Sonkajärvi, Finland

• Moscow, Russia
• Stalin's World, Lithuania

nsk,
larus
• Pripyat Amusement Park, Ukraine
• Enerhodar, Ukraine
• Ulaanbaatar, Mongolia

• Rebirth Island, Russia
Kazantip, The Crimea

Taahirojima Cat
• Beijing, China • Island, Japan
• • Tyrnavos, Greece
Suwon, South Korea •

Kavos, Greece
• Komaki, Japan

Kunming, China
Bhangarh, India •
Modern Toilet Restaurant •

• Cambodia

• Eyl, Somalia

Nambour, Australia •

Desolation Island •

WELCOME TO THE

TRISTAN DA CUNHA
SOUTH ATLANTIC

REMOTEST ISLAND

CHAPTER 1

MIDDLE OF NOWHERE

"...lost technology causes ships' systems to malfunction, pulling them deep into the sea."

DESOLATION ISLANDS

The name alone should give you an inkling of what to expect from this archipelago in the Indian Ocean. They're not really called the "Desolation Islands"—the official name is the Kerguelen Islands—but Desolation works better as the 300 islets are actually miles and miles away from any form of civilization.

If you're expecting a landscape of gray, rugged rock biting at the dreary skies above, and bizarre creatures that can be neatly filed under "abhorrence of nature" then you're in for a treat. The islands are bitterly cold all year round and it's always windy. In fact, it's so windy that butterflies—like the island's other insects—have evolved without wings. Anything airborne would simply be blown into the tempestuous sea and lost beneath the crashing waves, which on the plus side are surprisingly warm.

The islands, the largest oceanic landmass on Earth at 2,786 square miles, were visited by Captain Cook in 1776, and since then have been a popular destination for biologists and geologists. Like many oceanic land masses, the group of islands have no indigenous mammals or people, but there is a year-round presence of almost 110 scientists who work in the remote laboratories and satellite tracking centers that are based there.

Along with a missile silo, the French scientists are kept company by some of the animals that were previously taken there "to see how they get on"—rabbits, rats, deer, and cats. The rabbits have managed to wreck the eco-system, almost wiping out the native "cushion plants" and Kerguelen cabbage, while the reindeer are doing their best to eat all of the moss and lichen they can find. It is also possible to see rare breeds of sheep and cows that were being eaten to extinction in their native France.

HAITI

Anyone who thought that "Gone Till November" was the last they'd hear of The Fugee's Wyclef Jean had a horrible surprise when he suddenly reappeared on Shakira's "Hips Don't Lie." And, as if to prove to the world that he can—and will—appear at the worst possible moments, he made headlines again in 2010 with a wild bid to become the new Haitian president.

Of course, Wyclef's bid was rejected as, despite being born on the stricken island, he had left for New York when he was nine years old. To make matters worse, he couldn't speak either of the national languages (French or Creole), and his political aspirations were openly mocked by Sean Penn—which must have hurt.

In hindsight, even Wyclef might admit to having had something of a lucky escape, though. Haiti is the poorest country in the Western Hemisphere, and held that unenviable title even before the enormous 2010 earthquake that struck just miles from the capital, Port-au-Prince. Since the quake, which hit seven on the Richter Scale and was the worst in the region for 200 years, its population has been living in desperate conditions, with unclean water and poor sanitation raising the risk of contracting a serious disease.

Over half of Haiti's population of nine million people practises Voodoo, a shadowy religion often misunderstood by Westerners, but there are more sinister things to fear when visiting this Caribbean country. As Haiti struggles to get to its feet after the devastating disaster, violent crime has soared with robbery and kidnapping becoming endemic in the capital. It is advised to not even visit Haiti, with some holiday makers claiming they were robbed of their valuables before they'd even left the airport. Violent protests in Port-au-Prince occur regularly, stretching both the local and United Nations police forces that monitor the city. But despite all this hardship, the locals still feel thankful that they avoided having Wyclef as president.

BERMUDA TRIANGLE

The Bermuda Triangle is a byword for the weird, the dangerous, and the inexplicable. For years, experts and the general public have been intrigued and horrified by the sudden disappearance of boats and planes in the area between the Atlantic island of Bermuda, Puerto Rico, and Miami.

With no wreckage to help shape an explanation, theories have been pieced together from the final transmissions of terrified captains and pilots. One of the most chilling came from the flight leader of Flight 19, a group of five US Navy bombers on a training mission, whose final words were: "We are entering white water, nothing seems right. We don't know where we are, the water is green, no white."

While scientists are quick to dismiss ideas of supernatural occurrences, there are many people who believe the Bermuda Triangle to have an unearthly vibe. Some say it is the site of an electromagnetic anomaly that can affect navigation systems. Aerial pictures of the sea with unexplainable neon patches seem to support this theory.

One popular conspiracy theory is that the Triangle lies above the drowned city of Atlantis. There is no proof that Atlantis ever existed, but some claim that it is the energy waves from the dead city's lost technology that cause planes' and ships' systems to malfunction, pulling them deep into the sea.

Others claim that alien spaceships are abducting the vessels and their stricken crews, taking them back to their home planets to be studied and dissected.

However, experts tightly stand by the "most logical" answer: That no more ships sink in the Bermuda Triangle than they do anywhere else on the planet. The region is well known to have extreme tropical storms, and human error is often the reason for fatalities.

But they would say that, wouldn't they?

TRISTAN DA CUNHA

It's New Year's Eve. You're stuck on an island 2,000 miles away from civilization. There's a knock at the door. Gingerly you open it, only to be confronted by a gang of men in terrifying costumes screaming in your face. Welcome to Tristan da Cunha.

The world's remotest inhabited island is home to just 275 people—and some bizarre folk traditions acted out by the natives. Every year on December 31, or Old Year's Night as it is referred to locally, the young men of the island dress up in scary costumes and proceed to go door knocking with the sole aim of scaring women and children. They go by the name of the Okalolies, and ensure that every inch of their skin is covered, even their hands. These days, they wear the sort of gory latex masks you usually see at Halloween, but a few years ago they would've made crude costumes from animal skins—perhaps with a cow's tail as a beard.

They knock on doors, sometimes whooping or grunting, but never speaking, which adds to their sinister air of mystery. The householders invite them in, offering them refreshments, and then try to guess who is behind the disguise. If they're correct, the rumbled individuals have to remove their masks before heading to the next home for more drinks and guessing games. It's a highly treasured tradition, and the island's Government Administrator even hosts a special reception in their honor.

Another popular festival on Tristan da Cunha—which is a mere 1,750 miles away from South Africa, and a short paddle of 2,088 miles from Argentina—is Ratting Day, when the island's men set out at the break of day to try and catch as many rats and mice as possible. Working in teams, they unearth the hordes of vermin before catching them and slicing off their tails. The winning team is announced at the end of the day after all the tails have been counted, with further accolades given for the longest tail brought back.

While it might seem like an odd, medieval practice, Ratting Day helps decrease the amount of vermin that attack the islander's poultry and grain stocks, which is vital for the community's survival. Apparently, small children also relish the chance to learn how to find and eliminate rats' nests.

The whole day has a carnival atmosphere about it, with the women and elderly coming to join the brave hunters and their excited dogs for a lavish lunch on the plains. And after the day has ended, the party continues well into the night.

CHAPTER 2
NORTH AMERICA

"Why bother with the great outdoors when you can spend money on obnoxious machines that flash and screech at you until you feed them more coins?"

U.S.
POST OFFICE

NORTH POLE, ALASKA

If you thought it was just elves and a certain fat man in a red suit who lived at the North Pole, you're sorely mistaken. The small Alaskan city that shares its name with the enigmatic apex of the Earth—despite being 1,700 miles away from it—is home to people and animals other than reindeer. It's even home to an industry that isn't toy making; sadly it's in the shape of two oil refineries.

Of course, this would probably disappoint the Dahl and Gaske Development Company, who in 1952 gave the city its festive moniker because they wanted to attract toy manufacturers to the area. Previously it went by the rather more mundane name of Davis.

These days, inhabitants are confronted with red-and-white-striped, candy-cane-style street lights, and live on roads with such thoughtful, yet not particularly subtle, names as Snowman Lane, Kris Kringle Drive, Santa Claus Drive, and St. Nicholas Drive.

North Pole's boughs are decked with holly (and other decorations) the whole year round, and thousands of

Christmas-mad tourists flock to see its giant fiberglass Santa, which at 42 feet tall is the largest one in the world. It stands outside the Santa Claus House, a gift shop that, as December nears, receives thousands of letters from parents who want a North Pole postmarked letter addressed to their little snotty-nosed darling to drop on their doormat in anticipation of the festive season.

A town built on the spirit of Christmas might seem charming, but beneath the tinsel and novelty music lies a more sinister undertone. A Columbine-style school massacre plot was foiled in 2006, and a disagreement between the city's mayor and Senator John McCain over a comment he made about elves saw the latter receive a lump of coal in the post.

But it's not all gift-wrapped bile. Iconic TV artist Bob Ross lived in the area for many years, and claimed he found the jaw-dropping landscapes that surround North Pole to be a great source of inspiration for many of his "watch-as-he-goes" paintings.

EVANSVILLE, INDIANA

If you're fretting about not being trim enough for a trip abroad, then perhaps consider Evansville as your destination. A recent poll declared it to be America's fattest city, so you'll fit right in—or perhaps feel supermodel thin as you wrestle for space on the sidewalk with a rotund local.

The city is situated on the beautiful Ohio River where the states of Illinois and Kentucky meet, and was once known as the River City. But these days it's more likely you'll see a

stream of wheezing fatties crossing your field of vision as they laboriously clomp through the streets.

A 2011 poll revealed that almost 40 per cent of people in the Evansville region boasted a BMI of 30 or more, a figure that rates them as morbidly obese. Locals were incensed, and took a break from eating onion rings and huge burgers to declare that they're "happy!"

26

If you're able to stomach the sight of chubby arms oozing out of vest tops like molten wax, or the constant peril of almost being mown down by a hungry-looking blimp on a mobility scooter, there is much to do here. Like visit one of the city's many fast food restaurants. Or drive through burger joints. Or call for a pizza.

Failing that you could take a trip to the annual Fall Festival, which takes place in the first week of October. Described by organizers as "the largest street fair outside of Mardi Gras," it's a celebration of everything edible—as long as it's battered. You thought Scotland's deep-fried Mars Bars were bad for you? Wait until you've tried chicken-fried bacon, fried cheesecake on a stick, or deep-fried hotdogs.

One aspect of Evansville living that the locals are keen to remind everyone of is the fact that they enjoy some of the lowest energy rates in America.

Perfect for powering a microwave.

Ding!

CELEBRATION, FLORIDA

Disney films, so lurid they make you want to vomit salty tears of submission down your cheeks, are loved by children and adults alike. While the latter can often fob off their weakness for movies starring fairies, CGI cowboys, and singing lions as a by-product of their kid being such a huge fan, it may be a little bit harder to explain owning a load of Disney merchandise.

Of course, some grown-ups are perfectly happy to stride around their local town center with a gurning mouse plastered across their chest, or serve tea from an Aristocats teapot, but many prefer to keep their soft spot for Mulan on the DL—and who can blame them? It's really not cool.

So, how amazing that cartoon aficionados with a wad of cash burning in their pocket can invest in property in Celebration, the Florida town that is meant to bring Walt Disney's Experimental Prototype Community of Tomorrow (EPCOT) to life. Located just 10 minutes' drive from the Disney World resort, the town's 7,500 inhabitants are directly connected to the Magic Kingdom and enjoy a community spirit that has been described as "the return to small town values."

Beauty and the Beast fans may be disappointed to know that a morning trip to buy bread won't result in a mass town singalong, but as your neighbors are likely to be Disney fans you could try singing at them and seeing if they respond.

Residential areas have a "Caribbean flavor" and are usually painted a shade of pink, green, orange, or blue. The town's key buildings were designed by leading architects including Michael Graves and helped earn Celebration the title of the "Urban Land Institute's New Community of the Year" in 2001.

But it's not only its look which is sickly sweet. It's also been described as "like the town in Stepford Wives"—which, considering its townsfolk pride themselves on smiling at everyone, getting to know one another, and being super neighborly, might be less of a slur and more of a warning...

HELL, MICHIGAN

Welcome to Michigan, where, "I'll see you in Hell!" can literally mean just that. No one is sure how the town got its name, but some say a pair of German tourists visited in 1830 and said "So schön hell!" and the name just stuck. It is unlikely the locals realized it translated as "So beautifully bright!" Another theory is that the town's founder, George Reeves, was asked what the town was called and he snapped, "You can call it Hell for all I care!"

Hell has been engulfed by melodrama ever since, but never more so than in 2006 when the town's self-appointed mayor and gift shop manager, John Colone, declared June 6 a day of demonic revelry for the townsfolk (or Hellbillies as they're known) and devilish pilgrims.

On 6-6-06, souvenirs were slashed in price to $6.66, whether it be a mug, T-shirt, or the deeds to a square inch of Hell. The entrance to the children's play area was also given a revamp, with two enormous gates standing five feet across and eight feet wide installed. Each gate was designed to look like flames, and when closed they depicted a devil's head.

Despite there not being much to see or do in Hell, people enjoy visiting the town so they can tell their friends they've "been to Hell and back." One couple is even said to have made the most of the BYOB chapel so they could say they got married on a cold day in Hell.

CLEVELAND, OHIO

*New York is known as "The Big Apple,"
Tampa as "The Cigar Capital of the World,"
and poor old Cleveland is the "Mistake on
the Lake."*

Plonked on the edge of Lake Erie, Cleveland earned its less than impressive moniker by having a declining economy, little social or political influence, an exodus of residents, and a number of unsuccessful sports teams. In fact, the last time one of Cleveland's major teams won a trophy, Beatle Mania was sweeping the US and man was still five years away from landing on the moon.

So far, so depressing. Visit Ohio's second largest city and you're unlikely to be laughing much—or see anyone else in a particularly good mood for that matter, as Cleveland has an unemployment rate of 17.1 per cent, compared to the national average of 6.9 per cent. At least there isn't so much of a cocaine problem these days—but that's only because more people are turning to heroin. What perfect vices in the hometown of the Rock and Roll Hall of Fame!

Another title Cleveland holds is as one of the most dangerous cities in the United States—but even here it can't manage to claim a spot worthy of your fear and respect, ranking just outside the top 10 at number 11. Poor Cleveland.

Those who haven't yet made a bee-line for the exit can't even be placated by the weather. Summers are humid and winters bitter; it's not uncommon for the city to be blanketed by up to five feet of snow. Luckily the local cuisine is sure to make you feel better. How about some delicious stuffed cabbage served by the city's Central European community?

Is it any surprise that one of Cleveland's most famous residents, singer Eric Carmen, penned "All By Myself," one of the most depressing songs ever written?

BORING, MARYLAND

America is not a nation renowned for its understanding of the concept of irony, so when visiting Boring, Maryland, don't expect a surge of adrenaline. If sniggering at things is your idea of fun, then you'll enjoy pointing at the Boring Methodist Church, Boring Post Office, and the Boring Volunteer Fire Company, which also hosts games of bingo six nights a week.

Just because it's boring doesn't mean there aren't things to do, however. In June, the volunteer fire department hosts the Boring Gas Engine Show and Flea Market. It's a great opportunity to buy other people's junk and look at tractors, as well as gas and steam engines from 100 years ago. Such activities could never be considered dull.

The town took its name from its original Postmaster, David Boring. Such is his legacy—and one can imagine the overall sense of thankfulness to the postal system that their town even exists—that one of the most popular pastimes in the tiny community of just 40 houses is to visit the ancient postal station. It's now housed in the general store, which also doubles up as a great place to have your photo taken.

People have (apparently) flocked from as far away as South Africa just to be snapped next to the sign that reads "Boring." To be honest, if traveling all that way to have their photo taken next to a sign saying Boring is all they can come up with it's probably the best place for them.

CAVE-IN-ROCK, ILLINOIS

One of Illinois' top geological points of interest is Cave-in-Rock. It is literally a cave in a rock. If its walls could speak, they might tell you about the bandits, counterfeiters, and outlaws that used to hide there during the 18th century. They then might confide that those olden-days scumbags weren't a patch on the Insane Clown Posse fans who hang out there these days.

Every summer, trailers, cars spray-painted with clown faces, and rusty pick-up trucks from all over the United States head to Cave-in-Rock for the annual Gathering of the Juggalos festival. Spread across four days, over 100,000 horror-rap-loving pilgrims descend on the historical bolt hole for a long weekend of live music, autograph signing sessions, karaoke, wrestling, and wild partying.

The event is described as "Woodstock for Juggalos," but don't be fooled. There's no summer of love vibes here; just hoards of rednecks dressed like demented, big-top funny men spraying fizzy drinks over one another and yelling "woop woop!"

Internationally regarded as oddballs, Juggalos—along with their female counterparts who are known as Juggalettes—live their lives by the teachings of their evil clown heroes. They paint their faces into a distorted clown grimace, braid their hair so it looks like spiders' legs, and throw gang signs at one another. In fact, they love throwing gang signs so much that the FBI has labeled Juggalos a "loosely organized hybrid gang."

Do you really want to be enjoying a relaxing picnic with your family, only for some buck-toothed buffoon to storm over, steal the bottle of fizzy pop you're about to drink from, and spray it all over your wife and baby? If not, then you might want to give Cave-In-Rock a wide berth during these four days of madness.

VULCAN, CANADA

A singular Star Trek fan is manageable. Should they decide to start regurgitating quotes like, "our neural pathways have become accustomed to your sensory input patterns," it's quite easy to make them snap out of it by threatening to burn a signed picture of William Shatner or simply by applying some good old-fashioned brute force.

But what if the tables were turned and you were outnumbered 50 to one by Trekkies? How would you cope with being surrounded by people who can switch between English and Klingon at a moment's notice?

If you don't want to know, then don't go to Vulcan.

The Canadian farming town decided to cash in on its intergalactic namesake by building a giant replica of the

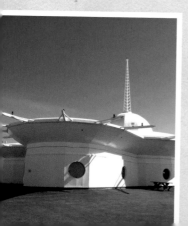

Starship Enterprise by the side of the highway, and has since become a prime holiday destination for hoards of sci-fi lovers. It's been pointed out that the two places have a similar climate (little rainfall with hot summer days and cool nights),

but the similarities don't end there. A never-ending supply
of pointy plastic ears also means that the Earth-based
Vulcans look the part too.

Vulcan is also home to the unique Vulcan Tourism and Trek
Station. Designed to look like a landing spaceship, its
interior is dominated by a floor-to-ceiling space mural
designed to make you feel like you have left Earth
altogether. Along with rooms of rare memorabilia, you also
have the opportunity to have your photo taken with
cardboard cutouts of the iconic crew of the Starship
Enterprise past and present. And don't worry if you
"accidentally" left your costume at home—they'll happily
lend you one.

BEEBE, ARKANSAS

Birdwatchers wanting to get closer to their feathered friends should pay a visit to Beebe. For two years in a row, January 1 has seen the streets of the Arkansas town littered with thousands of dead birds—and no one really knows why...

On December 31, 2010, more than 3,000 red-winged blackbirds and European starlings seemed to fall from the sky. Their corpses were found solely in a one-mile area, which added considerably to the eeriness of the mass death. Scientists conducted autopsies and concluded that the physical trauma found on the birds was consistent with being caught in a lightning or hail storm.

Neither of those had taken place that night, so the Arkansas Game and Fish Commission decided the birds had died as the result of a local resident setting off professional grade fireworks. They had startled the birds and caused them to panic and fly in to the night sky—with horrifying consequences.

The town imposed a fireworks ban the following year, but still an estimated 5,000 birds were found dead in Beebe on New Year's Day. Hours before, local television stations had reported a "black mass" over the town before the creatures once again dropped dead from the sky.

The Internet is rife with theories about these bizarre incidents, with electromagnetism being the favorite cause. Local residents and people counting down the days until the apocalypse bicker in Internet forums about what really went on. Some blame the seven different radio towers in Beebe that service private and commercial cell phone providers. Others claim it's down to the HAARP Project, a shady government initiative that is said to be able to cause earthquakes and change weather patterns by shifting the frequencies of radio waves.

Of course, the most popular reason is that the world is coming to an end and Satan will soon reign over all humanity!

JERSEY SHORE, NEW JERSEY

Before 2009, the Jersey Shore would have meant little to anyone who didn't reside in one of the 50 communities that line the 127 miles of New Jersey coastland overlooking the Atlantic Ocean. The area was widely regarded as a family holiday hotspot due to its clean beaches and close proximity to both New York and Pennsylvania. Mum and Dad got some fresh air, the kids could wear themselves out at the funfair, and teens could embark upon innocent holiday romances.

These days, however, it's synonymous with the MTV reality show of the same name that follows the jaw-dropping exploits of six Italian American twentysomethings who love nothing more than embracing their inner guido.

Distinguishable by their year-round tans, toned and muscular bodies, overly gelled hair, lack of common sense, barely there outfits, love of diamantes, and willingness to fight anyone that crosses their path, the motley crew have become a global sensation, with

audiences fascinated by the lives of J-Woww, Sammy Sweetheart, Pauly D, Ronnie, Vinny, pint-sized guidettes Deena and Snooki, and stomach-churning abs-flasher The Situation.

But not everyone is a fan. They are openly loathed by Italian American groups who consider their behavior and the way they have embraced the once derogatory term "guido" to be shameful. And they may have a point: TV cameras have captured the gang getting arrested, fighting, crying, screaming at each other, sleeping around, and fist pumping all night long to some incredibly tacky house music. They give the locals one night off from their madcap antics each week, when they instead stay in and spout moronic philosophy at each other as they enjoy a traditional Italian "family meal" of meatballs.

Amazingly, a large number of people have taken the guido mantra of "GTL" (gym, tan, laundry) firmly to heart, and the

Jersey Shore hub of Seaside Heights where the show is set has benefited greatly. Figures reveal that its population more than doubles in the summer, rising from 30,000 to 65,000 as young people from all over the region flock to the Shore to embrace the guido

lifestyle and get wasted at the scores of nightclubs offering cheap booze and horrendous rave music.

Should you find yourself on a New Jersey dancefloor surrounded by guidos, don't panic—they are easily placated if you reduce yourself to their level. The quickest way to do this is to crouch down and start thumping the floor with your fist. As the beat grows, so should your fist-pumping action until you are leaping up and down on the spot while cheering and trying to make sure your giant sunglasses don't fall off your face. The next stage is to find either a guidette or "gorilla juice head" to "smush." Just make sure you lay an old towel down first—fake tan can really stain.

ANTHROCON, PITTSBURGH, PENNSYLVANIA

When children see someone dressed up in an animal costume their first instinct is to run toward them with their arms outstretched, their face a giant beacon of joy ready for a quick cuddle. The same can be said of "furries"—adults who have a fixation with humanoid animal characters.

There are many Furry Conventions—or Fur Cons, as they're also known—held every year across the US. Such gatherings provide a suitable opportunity for furry fetishists to show off their "fursonas," the name given to their animal alter-egos who are usually only given the chance to socialize in Internet forums. The largest of these conventions is Anthrocon, which is held every year in Pittsburgh, Pennsylvania, and attended by over 4,000 people who roam around as humanoid cats, dogs, wolves, and even cockroaches. Foxes are also popular.

Many of the furries wear full costumes that they have painstakingly made themselves, while others opt for a more subtle get-up, such as attaching a discreet tail to their clothes or wearing gloves that look like paws. The furries' outfits help to portray their character, with some having a medieval mentality that involves wearing fantasy outfits like cloaks and tunics, while others in appear in uniforms or more relaxed clothing such as dungarees.

Thousands of furry fans make the most of Anthrocon, relishing the chance to hang out with other people in animal suits and dancing all night at specially organized discos, where any records by the rock band Super Furry Animals go down especially well. It's also a chance to bring their online role-playing games to life, as they speak and act in character totally unlike their everyday personas. It's not all fun and games, though, as the more serious side of the fandom is explored in a series of panel discussions. There are also art shows, auctions, puppetry, and stalls selling comic books, accessories, collectables, and, of course, animal costumes.

Getting into a Fur Con can be tricky, however, as the media has painted such events as sexually charged weekends that culminate in wild orgies; as a result, the furries are understandably wary of outsiders. Make an effort, though, and perhaps you'll see a grinning six-foot-tall crocodile slide up to a mouse, take them by the paw, and lead them to a hotel suite with the intention of doing beastly things to them.

WEIRS BEACH, NEW HAMPSHIRE

Do people go to Weirs Beach to admire the tranquil scenery of Lake Winnipesaukee? Do they want to while away the days on some of New Hampshire's beautiful sandy beaches, roaming casually through the lush vegetation that encases its shore, or spend hours kayaking with only their thoughts for company? Nope, they go to play video games.

Why bother with the great outdoors when you can spend your hard-earned money on obnoxious machines that flash and screech at you until you feed them more coins? Who needs nature!

Weirs Beach is the home of Funspot, the World's Largest Arcade. It features over 500 video games, indoor golf, a 20-lane bowling center, bingo hall, a restaurant, and a tavern. The third floor is home to the American Classic

Arcade Museum, which always has at least 180 games from the seventies and eighties for you to get your hands on; basically it's the geek equivalent of a Roman orgy.

Just in case those 700-odd video games aren't enough to tire your thumbs out, the Half Moon Arcade is also located nearby. According to its website—last updated in 1999!—it has a Penny Arcade, Family Fun Center, and bumper cars.

The bumper cars aren't the only vehicles you'll see in Weirs Beach, though. It's also a popular place for bikers, who have been coming to the area since 1916 to, um, ride their motorbikes around (and probably have a game of Mortal Kombat or two). In the summer, bikers and petrol heads arrive for Laconia Motorcycle Week, seven whole days of riding, racing, and drinking that officially kickstart the summer season.

So if you like your areas of outstanding natural beauty to reverberate with bleeps, the jangling of coins, and the unmistakable heavy roar of a Harley Davidson, you'll simply love Weirs Beach. Similarly, if you've ever wanted to see the fear in a translucent-skinned nerd's eyes as he accidentally knocks into a hairy biker's "hog," then you'll simply love Weirs Beach.

EAST DUBLIN, GEORGIA

As if hosting the Olympics wasn't enough of a chore, the organizers of the 1996 games in Atlanta had to deal with a load of redneck jokes as well. One group of locals was inspired by the scorn poured on their locale, however, and decided it would be funny to host their own alternative competition: the Summer Redneck Games.

It was such a success that it now takes place every year, with all profits going to charity. Thousands of people flock to East Dublin every summer to soak up the atmosphere and cheer and whoop for their favorite redneck competitors, but the fun doesn't officially start until the ceremonial grill has been lit by a local man named L-Bow. This toothless individual, in his grubby overalls and threadbare shoes, is the games' unofficial mascot.

The sports are weird and wonderful, and range from odd to downright disgusting. There's Hubcap Tossin', Redneck Horseshoes (which involves throwing toilet seats), and the gag-inducing Bobbing For Pigs' Trotters. Some sports are less about physical skill and more about just having a good aim, such as Watermelon Seed Spitting and Bug Zappin' By Spitball, whatever that means.

Ladies can enter a Wet T-shirt Competition, as well as another contest for the Biggest Hair. But, rednecks being rednecks, you know the men will have a mullet that's just as impressive as the hairstyles of their lady-friends, as well as some incredible moobs. All winners get to take home a special trophy—a half-crushed beer can mounted on a plinth.

One of the highlights of the day-long event is the Armpit Serenade, where youngsters try their hardest to use their hands and armpits to "fart" the tunes of famous songs. With such beautiful music filling the air, is it any surprise that romance blossoms at the Redneck Summer Games? One year, Rawni and Rob Sprague chose it as the place for their wedding. They now return every year to celebrate their anniversary by being the first to take part in the Mud Pit Belly Flop.

CHAPTER 3
THE PACIFIC

"Days later, police discovered burnt remains and teeth in a clearing in the forest."

PITCAIRN ISLAND

Tentatively bracing the balance between idyllic and inbred is Pitcairn Island. Located roughly halfway between New Zealand and Peru, the entire population of the island is descended from the mutineers from the HMS Bounty who arrived in 1789 and set up home with some Tahitians they had kidnapped. Since this initial landing, the island's population has grown from six men, 11 women, and a baby, to a grand total of 48.

The extreme isolation of the island has resulted in a largely interrelated population of four families—Christian, Warren, Young, and Brown—while a high profile pedophilia trial in 2004 revealed some of the more sinister undertones of "island life."

If that hasn't put you off, the mere act of getting there is a nightmare in itself. A flight from Los Angeles, Auckland, or Tokyo will take you to Tahiti, from where a small plane will carry you to Mangareva in the Gambier Islands, after which a 300 mile boat journey awaits. The Claymore II carries supplies and passengers to Pitcairn every three months and docks at the remote destination for a maximum of one week.

It's crucial to take plenty of cash to Pitcairn as there are no ATMs. The official currency is New Zealand dollars, but you'll need US dollars to buy any souvenirs. There aren't actually any souvenir shops, but the islanders make knick-knacks that they'll happily sell to you from their homes.

Activity-wise, you can dive in the crystal blue waters and explore the wrecks of the SS Cornwallis and the boat that started it all, the HMS Bounty. You could stroll up the invitingly named Hill of Difficulty or celebrate Bounty Day on January 23 by helping the locals burn an effigy of the infamous ship. The tourist board also cite chopping down a banana tree, basket weaving and wood carving as other fun activities to enjoy during your stay.

The local dialect, Pitkern, is a unique blend of 18th-century English and Tahitian. That's why "Ye like-a sum whettles?" means, "Would you like some food." If you do, then head to Christian's Café from 6:30pm on a Friday—because that's the only option available.

NUKU HIVA, FRENCH POLYNESIA

Until the summer of 2011, Nuku Hiva was merely a paradise isle in French Polynesia. With a population of 2,000, acres of beautiful rainforests, clear blue skies, and glistening seas to match, it was a destination for honeymooners and explorers alike. German adventurer Stefan Ramin fell in to the latter category, and stopped off at the 127 square mile island while on a three-year sailing trip around the world with his girlfriend Heike Dorsch.

Upon arrival, they met Henri Haiti, a local man who offered to be their guide. Stefan accompanied him for a day of goat hunting in the dense forest. After many hours, Henri arrived back at the couple's camp, claiming that Stefan had been injured in the forest and asking Heike to accompany him back to the scene of the "accident." When she refused, she told local police that he tied her to a tree and tried to assault her. Heike eventually managed to escape and raise the alarm, but by that time Henri had vanished back into the undergrowth, and there was still no sign of Stefan to be found anywhere.

Days later, police discovered burnt remains and teeth in a clearing in the forest. German dental records proved they belonged to the missing explorer, and the awful realization that he had been eaten by his guide began to sink in. The authorities continue to hunt for Henri, who is thought to have cocooned himself in the island's unwelcoming natural habitat in an attempt to evade capture.

Suddenly, age-old prejudices of island cannibalism rose to the surface. Locals were furious, claiming that these days the island's 2,000-strong population prefer eating hotdogs to people. Evidently, it seems that one of them fancied a bite of a Frankfurter that day.

NAMBOUR, AUSTRALIA

Australia's a big country, so is it any surprise it's home to a big pineapple? And it's not just any old big pineapple, but the biggest one in the entire world.

Just a few miles away from Brisbane and standing an enormous 52 feet high, the world's biggest pineapple has been thrilling tourists and fruit fans since 1971 who, after walking up its internal spiral staircase, love to take in the stunning vistas from beneath its static green plume.

Until the summer of 2011 it looked like the Big Pineapple would be left to rot at the side of the road, however. It had fallen in to disrepair, and many feared for its future. Luckily, three local businessmen clubbed together to buy it—along with the 406 acre plot it stands on—for a cool AUS $5.8 million.

Now they're working hard to restore the Big Pineapple to its former

glory, as well as reinvigorating the fruit farm it once called home. Families used to laugh with glee as they boarded the farm's Sugar Cane Train for an educational ride that showed them the fruits of Queensland, surrounding them with over 100 varieties of plants and giving special focus to the golden pineapples that the region is famous for.

There was also a koala sanctuary on the site, along with a petting zoo and animal nursery where you could get up close and personal with various different forms of wildlife. Doesn't it sound idyllic? There was even a Nutmobile that would take you on an awe-inspiring journey through macadamia plantations and lush rainforests.

Tragically, these days it's just a giant fiberglass pineapple by the side of the road.

CHAPTER 4

ASIA

"...On day eight of the gridlock, trucks moved less than a mile—an average speed of under 66 meters an hour."

"Try insects like grubs, cockroaches, and worms, or a bowl of fried sparrow and rice."

ULAN BATOR, MONGOLIA

It's one of those countries that you sometimes have to question the reality of, but Mongolia is very, very real. In the center of this landlocked Asian country is Ulan Bator, the capital city that almost 45 per cent of the entire Mongolian population call home.

Its unique geographical position, in a valley located over 4,400 feet above sea level, makes Ulan Bator—or UB as the locals call it—one of the most isolated cities on Earth. As if this wasn't unlucky enough, its high-up position, distance from any coast, and Siberian weather anomalies mean that UB is also the coldest capital city in the world, with a climate that is almost subarctic.

The 2.8 million residents experience only brief warm summers before being plunged back into bitterly cold winters, with temperatures regulalrly falling below the -20 degrees Fahrenheit mark in January and February. Winter also means less than four hours of sunlight a day, with two hours being a lucky occurrence during December.

Despite the gloom that descends over Ulan Bator in the winter months, and the smog that is belched out by the newly industrialized city (some residents sarcastically call it "Utaanbaatar," which translates as "smog hero"), visitors can enjoy sights including historic Buddhist temples and monasteries, bold statues that hint at the country's communist past, and some beautiful architecture.

After dark, the city's hedonistic reputation can be explored by embarking on a bar and club crawl. Just be careful not to bump into anyone on the dancefloor as this could trigger a mass brawl, and be sure not to get caught drinking on the streets unless you want to be arrested and made to spend the night in a drunk tank.

KUNMING, CHINA

Queuing for hours to get on a ride at a theme park only to get to the front and be told you're too short is a rite of passage that many people go through. But that's unlikely to happen at China's latest attraction, which goes by the name of Dwarf Kingdom. Here, you'll be entertained by 80 dwarves who have traveled from across the country to live and work in a place where they won't be harassed or bullied as a result of their diminutive stature.

Each day, they entertain the scores of tourists who arrive at the park, excited to see the little people perform slapstick comedy routines and putting on an all-singing, all-dancing show to remember.

The "king" dwarf is the shortest member of the troupe, barely clearing two-feet in height. He struts about like a hen-high peacock, a yellow military-style coat emblazoned with mushrooms, and a pair of wrap-around sunglasses hinting at his top-dog status. His colleagues, none taller than four feet, dress like hip-hop gangsters, medieval soldiers, butterflies, and cooks.

There's no denying that there's a jovial atmosphere as the little people shimmy, body pop, and dance for their applauding audience during the two daily shows. After the final curtain the residents of Dwarf Kingdom keep smiling as they pose for photographs with grinning tourists and prepare over-priced hot drinks in one of the resort's three faux-castles. At night they stay on site, returning to their pint-sized homes which bear an uncanny resemblance to the cartoon toadstools where The Smurfs lived.

Years of bad treatment have nevertheless left many of the little people with short fuses and fearsome fighting skills, however. Not only have scuffles broken out among the workers, but there have also been cases of gangs of little people sneaking out of the park at night and heading in to nearby towns to smash up their "normal-sized" rivals. One fight was apparently so bloody that a dwarf lost his job as a result.

And that's a tall story you wouldn't expect from the world's only midget theme park, is it?

BEIJING, CHINA

If roadtrips are your thing it's safe to say Beijing is maybe not the best place to start. Congestion is pretty higher at the best of times, but in 2010 the outskirts of Beijing saw one of the world's worst traffic jams. It stretched over 62 miles in length and lasted an astounding 11 days.

Essential road works were needed to repair the damage caused by heavy lorries bringing coal into the city along the Beijing-Tibet Expressway, meaning that it was these same lorries that made up most of the traffic, along with some understandably annoyed commuters.

Furious drivers were trapped on a stretch of road between Jining in Inner Mongolia and Huai'an in Hebei Province, north-west of Beijing. Tensions ultimately ran so high that 400 police officers were dispatched to patrol the area.

Not only did they have to keep an eye out for the drivers' welfare, they also had to make sure there were no fights between people stuck in the traffic and shrewd salesmen who had come to sell noodles, tea, and other useful items, albeit at significantly increased prices. These salesmen would go from vehicle to vehicle, or even set up stalls beside the road in order to reap the benefits of their captive audience.

As the days passed faster than anything with wheels, people began socializing with each other and playing cards or chess on the roadside. Requests were made for bands to come and perform on the verges to quell boredom. People were nevertheless forced to sleep in their cars, with some clocking up five nights before either making a detour or reaching their exit. On day eight of the gridlock, trucks moved less than a mile on the worst-hit section of the expressway—an average speed of under 66 meters an hour.

CAMBODIA

Several hours' drive from the Cambodian capital of Phnom Penh is the village of Skuon, also known by the rather less inviting name of "Spiderville" as a result of the locals' penchant for an eight-legged snack. Arachnids first found themselves on the menu during the Khmer Rouge years when food was scarce, but were deemed so delicious that they have remained a part of Cambodian cuisine ever since.

The palm-sized tarantulas are bred in holes in the ground in nearby villages, or foraged for in forestland. Once caught, they are seasoned with a mixture of MSG, sugar, salt, and crushed garlic before being fried in oil.

The chefs know they're cooked when "the legs are almost completely stiff, by which time the contents of the abdomen are not so runny." It is not totally clear if the abdomen is really edible—it does after all contain organs, feces, and sometimes eggs—but some regard the brown paste that oozes out of the spider to be a delicacy; others, somewhat understandably, disagree. The legs contain little flesh but the head and body have a "delicate" white meat inside that is said to taste like a cross between chicken and cod.

A trip to the capital's Phsar Thmey market is a chance to browse stalls selling some of Cambodia's other equally outrageous dishes. Try fried insects like grubs, cockroaches, and worms or a bowl of deep-fried sparrow and rice.

Maybe offal is more your thing and you fancy animal stomach, monkey brains, or a deep-fried embryonic chick? Similarly, why not try balut, which is a duck foetus that has been boiled alive in its egg.

Cambodians also think that frogs make a great snack, and the poor creatures can often be found skinned but still hopping around. Snakes on skewers, dog meat, and rats are also everyday dishes.

If you need to get in the right frame of mind to eat some of the local delicacies, however, a slice of "happy pizza" might help. The way the chefs swap oregano for marijuana means you'll have such a bad case of the munchies that you'll probably eat anything.

SUWON, SOUTH KOREA

The youth of South Korea have a strange hobby that involves collecting models and stickers of "cute poops"—basically turds with happy smiling faces. The trend even extends to food if you've ever fancied the idea of buying cakes and donuts that are designed to look like edible feces.

Dongchimee is a popular Korean cartoon character who uses his own "dung" to make art. His name is taken from the popular game of dong chimm, which is when a child sneaks up on an adult and tries to stick their two index fingers up their backside. Dong chimm roughly translates as "poop needle."

With such an emphasis on excrement, it's no surprise that, as a nation, South Korea is obsessed with toilets. While most public lavatories require you to squat over a hole in the ground (and bring your own toilet paper), there are also some really futuristic, hi-tech ones available.

It's not uncommon to hear of Westerners being left totally bemused by a remote-controlled toilet with 12 different settings and no flush in sight. Jets of water spray out, perfume is puffed into the stall, a hairdryer replaces the need for toilet paper, and gentle music is played to hide any tell-tale sounds of bodily functions.

In Suwon, less than 30 miles south of Seoul, you can visit a museum dedicated to porcelain thrones. The building itself is shaped like a toilet, and was once the home of Sim Jae-Duck, chairman of the Inaugural General Assembly of the World Toilet Association. The eccentric Korean even claimed he was born in a toilet.

The 4,508 square foot, $1.6 million toilet house was built in 2007, and is called "Mr. Toilet's House." Visitors flock to the impressive building to learn more about toilets, and also to use the toilet, which is the bizarre museum's main attraction. But make a visit to this unique attraction and you won't just be flushing your money down the toilet—all profits go toward providing good-quality public amenities in underdeveloped countries.

BHANGARH, INDIA

In 1783 the city of Bhangarh was suddenly abandoned overnight—and no one knows exactly why. Widely regarded as India's most haunted city, the fear that surrounds this ancient palace and the buildings located near it is no less acute now than it was 200 years ago.

Legend has it that a wicked magician called Singhia Sevra condemned the city and its inhabitants to death without rebirth. It is widely regarded as one of the most haunted places in the world, and definitely the most cursed place in India.

It is said that no one who stays after dark makes it out alive, and it is actually illegal to be in Bhangarh after the sun sets. An official government notice at the entrance to the city is a stark warning that it's a dangerous place once it gets dark. It reads: "Important warning: Entering the borders of Bhangarh before sunrise and after sunset is strictly prohibited. Anyone flouting the rules mentioned above will face legal action."

Whether this is to deter looters and vandals or because of something more sinister is unknown. Visitors claim to be overwhelmed with a sense of unease when roaming the ruins, which stretch for miles and include two Hindu temples, a fort, and 10,000 dwellings.

Locals claim that the fort's basement has never been truly explored, apart from one brave person who descended the stairs, never to return. Others say that they have heard voices and seen fresh blood on the ground, even though the place is deserted. The general rumor is that the city "comes alive" at night, and you will never return should you find yourself there after dark.

The only life that exists in the city today are banyan trees, the odd rat, and a few troops of monkeys who aren't concerned by ghosts. Overlooking the haunted town is a lonely chhatri, which is said to contain the remains of Singhia Sevra, the occult priest that doomed Bhangarh.

HIME-NO-MIYA FESTIVAL, KOMAKI, JAPAN

"Come on kids, get ready, we're gonna be late for the vagina parade!" This isn't some sick fantasy, this is a quote from a Japanese parent getting their family ready to attend the Hime-no-miya grand vagina festival*.

Unlike a lot of fertility festivals that seem to focus on penises, the Japanese are happy to focus on women's bits, too. The Hime-no-miya festival is a sacred tradition that involves prayers, food, and general celebration. Would-be parents attend in the hope that the following year they will be returning with a baby and a reason to be thankful. It's not unusual for children and adults to wear themed costumes.

The festival begins with a group of children carrying a small vagina relic through the streets of Gakuden to the Ogata shrine. Later, a group of 40 men take the same route, carrying a giant vulva sculpture as part of a special parade. At the end, pink and white rice ball treats are hurled into the crowd.

Similarly, March 15 is Hōnen Matsuri, or harvest festival. This fertility festival is celebrated across the country, but the best known one happens in Komaki. The main attraction is an enormous 8-foot long wooden penis that snakes its way through the city streets to the Tagata shrine.

The festival is a chance for people to be thankful for a good harvest and pray for prosperity over the coming 12 months. It's also a great excuse to buy genital-shaped souvenirs—vagina ashtray anyone?—and eat penis-shaped confectionary.

What's really quite odd, however, is that there are shrines to vaginas and the chance to eat sweets shaped like penises in a country where erections in porn are censored.

*Probably

TASHIROJIMA CAT ISLAND, JAPAN

As odd as it seems, some folk simply don't like cats. Those people would definitely hate to find themselves stranded on Tashirojima, a small island off the coast of Japan that has more furry four-legged feline inhabitants than humans.

There are only around 100 people on Tashirojima, and most of them are over 70. The island's facilities are very limited—there are no ATMs, restaurants, or supermarkets, but there are seven inns. Dogs are banned from the island, but it nevertheless enjoys a steady stream of tourists eager to see the cats who, despite being feral, are still friendly.

The silk worm farmers who originally lived and worked on Tashirojima brought cats to the island a long time ago as they wanted them to keep the island's rodent population down. The cats did a fantastic job of nearly wiping out the silk worms' natural enemy,

and were soon enjoying scraps of fish and bits of seafood from the locals.

It wasn't long before the cats were a part of island life, their colony increasing in size year on year. People started carefully studying the creatures, noting their behavior and matching it to fishing conditions and changes in the weather.

It is said that a fisherman accidentally killed one of the cats once, and was so upset that he buried its body and built a small shrine called Neko Jinja. It still stands today, and is decorated with various knick-knacks and pebbles that have cats drawn on them by thrilled tourists.

Stone monuments of cats are dotted around the island, as are cat-shaped buildings designed by Shotaro Ishinomori, a premier Manga illustrator.

The islanders believe that feeding the cats will bring wealth and good fortune, and perhaps they're right: Cat Island survived the terrible tsunami that devastated the eastern coast of Japan in 2011.

MODERN TOILET RESTAURANT, TAIWAN

Dogs drink out of toilets, so why can't we? Well, unless you're doing it at the Taiwanese restaurant chain Modern Toilet, it's because you'll probably catch a horrible disease.

One of Taipei's best-loved restaurant chains, Modern Toilet, allows diners to fulfill their fantasies of eating chicken curry out of a porcelain throne and drinking the contents of a urinal through a straw.

The proprietors, or "muckrakers" as they call themselves, proclaim they live by the motto "In an age where creative marketing is king, even feces can be turned into gold!"

The first restaurant served chocolate ice cream which was piped into a small, toilet-shaped dish to look like a fresh

turd. Such was the positive reaction that they expanded their menu, and now offer a selection of hot meals as well.

The chicken curry is a popular option, but as it is served bubbling in its porcelain-throne vessel it may test the nerves of even the most ravenous customer.

The chain's flagship store is spread across 2,800 square feet and located over three storeys. An enormous toilet is fixed to the outside wall, and at the entrance a giant fiberglass poo awaits diners, ready to greet them with an anime grin. Patrons sit on Western-style toilets with glittery lids, and the tables are sinks or bathtubs with a glass top. The walls are tiled like a real bathroom, and the lights are shaped like luminescent piles of doo-doo.

The meals are served in mini-toilet bowls, mini-bathtubs, or mini-sinks. Giant desserts designed for sharing come in mini squat toilets, overflowing with nuts and chocolate sauce. Drinks are served in mini-urinals complete with a fun bendy straw.

Modern Toilet is a popular destination for hipsters, tourists, and children. There's even a gift shop where you can invest in your very own toilet-shaped dish, or a keyring shaped like—you've guessed it—a poo.

"...it's estimated that the pirates have been making up to US $30 million a year..."

CHAPTER 5
AFRICA

"...the Voodoo festival offers the chance to pick up dried animal corpses that are needed for luck."

EYL, SOMALIA

That Johnny Depp has a lot to answer for. His portrayal of Captain Jack Sparrow has made "pirate" a by-word for sexy and funny, when in reality they are anything but. It really would be interesting to see how he fared in Eyl, Somalia's pirate capital.

It is from here that the country's many pirate gangs operate and moor the stolen vessels for which they demand millions of dollars in ransom. The coastal town, located in the Puntland region, is heavily guarded, and has gradually developed from a simple port into a pirate paradise.

Amazingly, among the new ventures in the area are restaurants designed for feeding hostages and their

captors. After all, captives need to be fed—no one will pay for a dead sailor. The Somalis aboard the ships also need to be catered for, so, while you're relaxing on

the beach it isn't uncommon to see speed boats laden with meals whizzing off into the Gulf of Aden to make a dinner delivery.

No boat is safe from the ruthless Somali pirates—whether it's cargo from China, oil, or aid meant for their own country, the pirates will stop at nothing to snatch it. As a deterrent, warships from France, Canada, and Malaysia patrol the waters, but still the hijackings and intimidation continues.

It's estimated that the pirates have been making up to US $30 million a year, dwarfing the annual budget of Puntland which is no more than US $20 million. Evidence of this enormous stream of money can be seen in the form of mansions built throughout the region and a procession of fancy cars speeding along its roads. The pirates also continue to invest in high-grade weapons and powerful new boats which make them even more fearsome and harder to stop.

If you do decide to visit Ely, it's probably worth making sure you have enough spending money to double up as a ransom payment should things go awry.

FESTAC TOWN, NIGERIA

If you have an email address, chances are you've received an email from someone in Nigeria who has a huge amount of money that he needs stored somewhere safe, such as in your bank account. But first, won't you help him bribe government officials so he can fulfil his diplomat father's wishes and take a holdall of gold to Hamburg?

Every year, thousands of foolish people lose huge amounts of money to advance fee fraud, or "419 scams" as they're commonly known. But where do these badly written pleas come from? The answer is more often than not Festac Town, a suburb of the Nigerian capital Lagos.

Festac was originally built to house the participants in the Second World Festival of Black Arts and Culture in 1977. Five thousand homes were built in a neighborhood that was meant to represent a bright new age of prosperity for the country as it rode the crest of its first oil boom.

Until the late 1980s, Festac was a smart neighborhood, but as time went on it fell into disrepair and a new generation, educated but unemployed, moved in. They took advantage of the area's Internet cafés and began using e-scams to trick greedy Westerners.

Nigeria is ranked third in the fraudulent email crime statistics of the US Federal Agency's Internet Crime Complaint Center—pretty impressive for a country with less than 20 per cent Internet coverage.

Cybercrime is now a part of Nigerian culture, and home grown rapper Olu Maintain even had a hit record with "Yahooze," a track all about the high jinks of an email scammer, or "Yahoo Boys" as they call themselves.

While it could appear that an email asking you to send money to bribe someone or pay some sort of government levy is the behavior of a chancer, Yahoo Boys are usually part of a finely tuned organized crime syndicate—so the next time you're in Festac, keep an eye out for any new cars with an FST number plate. Chances are it's being driven by one of these unscrupulous online con-artists.

BENIN

The Western African country of Benin is renowned for two things: slaves and Voodoo. While slavery is no longer commonplace, Voodoo is, and two-thirds of Benin's nine million population openly practices it.

One of the country's most important cities is Ouidah. It was here that over one million Africans were brought to from across the continent, ready to be put on ships and sent across the world to work as slaves. Once in Ouidah they passed through the Porte du Non-Retour—the Door of No Return—as they were led in shackles to waiting vessels and an uncertain future.

But when they left, they took their Voodoo beliefs with them, some of which have thrived until the modern day, especially in countries such as Haiti.

Ouidah is regarded as the birthplace of Voodoo, and it is here that some of the religion's holiest sites can be found. A visit to this coastal city allows you to be immersed in the mysticism of Voodoo, and a walk around some of its holiest locations, including the Sacred Forest and the Temple of the Pythons, is an eye-opening experience.

In the Sacred Forest, which has only recently been opened to tourists, it's possible to see a tree that legend says used to be a king. At the Temple of the Pythons, snakes slither around freely, and goat and bird sacrifices still take place.

The city also plays host to an annual Voodoo festival. Every January, the streets are overflowing with pilgrims and tourists who arrive in their thousands to enjoy the vibrant atmosphere. The Voodoo belief system says the spirits of the dead live alongside the world of the living, and that they can be called on to help in times of need. The festival has a carnival atmosphere, with people wearing traditional costumes and robes to dance, play instruments, chant, and attend holy ceremonies.

As well as absorbing the culture, the Voodoo festival also offers you the chance to pick up "fetishes," dried animal corpses, and talismans that are needed for luck—or to put a curse on someone.

"Sadly, Stalin's World is not some sort of Disneyland for Marxists, nor a sort of "Clarissa Explains It All" with a USSR twist."

CHAPTER 6
EUROPE

"...most people visit since they believe Bugarach is situated at the base of an alien garage."

KAZANTIP, UKRAINE

Those wanting a tranquil break might want to avoid Ukraine's KaZantip. Lasting a marathon four weeks, the festival is one of the world's longest parties. But who would want to go to a month-long rave with 23 hours of trance music each day? According to the organizers, beautiful women and people who "believe that dreams come true, that impossible is nothing, and that people have no limits and can fly."

Over 150,000 "ParadiZers" flock to the Crimean coast every summer to see some of the world's biggest DJs and dance until they drop. Many revelers wear orange clothing, while others drag yellow suitcases behind them, making the festival look as loud as it sounds.

To enter KaZantip, which models itself as a republic, it is necessary to obtain a "Viza." This is valid for the duration of the festival, meaning you can leave and come back later if you want to give your eyes a rest from all the neon clothes.

Along with non-stop music and a beautiful coastline, another of the festival's main pulls are the thousands of beautiful women who "flock to KaZantip to be free, relax, party, make love, dance in the sun and under the moon." These women also attract hoardes of Ukranian crooks and Russian mafia, who come to splash the cash, get laid, and get wasted. In fact, it can seem at times as if half of Moscow has descended on the site as Russians claim August as holiday time.

If the vision of a pack of vicious beefcakes in designer sunglasses necking neat vodka from the bottle and flashing fistfuls of money in diamond-encrusted hands wasn't scary enough, there is also a weekly "Freak Parade." Anyone can join in as long as they're wearing something outrageous and are happy to prance around like an idiot.

The opening and closing parties are big events, with huge pyrotechnic shows and massive crowds of drunk people going berserk. Little is known about what happens once you're inside the vast KaZantip compound, but utopian ideas of free love and "dancing suspended in space and time" sound promising. If you meet the woman of your dreams, you can even marry her for the duration of the festival.

Adding to the madness is the KaZantip New Year on July 31. It's treated like a normal New Year's Eve with fireworks, champagne, and more hedonistic partying until sunrise.

STALIN'S WORLD, LITHUANIA

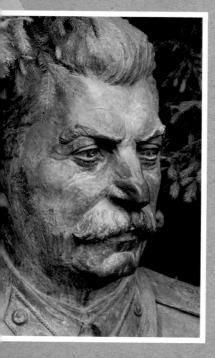

Sadly, Stalin's World is not some sort of Disneyland for Marxists, nor a sort of "Clarissa Explains It All" with a USSR twist, but the nickname of Grutas Park in Lithuania.

It's a sculpture park packed full of enormous monuments to long-dead red heroes. Spread over 500 acres, it features enormous statues of communist icons, including Vladimir Lenin, Joseph Stalin, and Karl Marx, as well as various Lithuanian politicians and Felix Dzerzhinsky, who organised the Red Terror.

There are nearly 90 statues of different shapes and sizes in the park, all of which could once be found in towns and cities across Lithuania.

The park was founded in 2001 by entrepreneur Viliumas Malinauskas, who also saw fit to ring it with razor wire and watch towers to give the place an authentic "gulag atmosphere." Morale boosting propaganda songs from the Soviet-era are also continuously blasted from loud speakers, urging tourists to work harder to make the USSR great once again .

Upon arrival, visitors can roam the grounds and admire the statues—some of which are over 30 feet high and weigh in excess of 75 tons—or take their children to one of the on-site playgrounds or the mini-zoo. Over 200,000 people visit the park every year, happily traipsing along the wooden walkways that link each exhibit. On special occasions, they are even treated to actors performing Soviet sponsored festivals from a by-gone era. The site also features a museum containing propaganda, photographs, and paintings.

Grutas Park has been met with mixed emotions from locals. Some see it as two-fingered salute to the country's 50-year

Soviet occupation, while others say it is an insult to the 300,000 people that were shipped off to Siberian prison camps for political dissent.

MOSCOW, RUSSIA

If rumors are to be believed, Moscow is awash with unsavory characters: oligarchs, lunatic taxi drivers, enraged Chechens, begging gipsies, Mafia bosses, KGB spies, beautiful but vindictive women, bent police looking for a bribe... the city is portrayed as a colorful yet frightening place.

But it's not the city's staggering 10.5 million population you really have to look out for, it's the 35,000 stray dogs that also call Moscow home.

The homeless hounds shelter anywhere and everywhere, from doorways to building sites. It's thought that around 500 stray dogs are even to be found living in the city's ornate Metro system and, of these, a small percentage has learnt how to commute to good begging areas.

It's rare to see a malnourished stray dog in Moscow, and they can actually afford to pick and choose what they eat. As well as learning how to use public transport, they have also been seen sending the cuter members of their packs to beg for food as they know they are more likely to be successful.

On the whole, the Muscovites and street dogs live harmoniously, with many residents leaving food out for them, and even building wooden shelters in their gardens so they can escape the cold Russian winters. In fact, there was

national outrage in 2001 when one of Moscow's most popular strays was stabbed to death by a commuter. Yulia Romanova was walking her pet dog through Mendeleyevska station when they were confronted by Malchik, which means "little boy" in Russian. The black mongrel had lived in the station for about three years, and was appreciated for guarding it against other dogs and drunks. Reports claim Malchik growled at Yulia's pet—so she pulled a kitchen knife out of her handbag and stabbed the poor animal to death.

Romanova was arrested and forced to undergo psychiatric treatment for a year. Locals were so upset about Malchik's grisly end that they clubbed together to have a statue of their fallen friend installed at the station. Today, people can be seen walking past the bronze dog and rubbing his nose for luck.

NORILSK, RUSSIA

Sometimes it's hard to find something nice to say about a place. Norilsk in Russia is definitely one such town—it's Siberia's most northern city, located snugly in the Arctic Circle, and well within the continuous permafrost zone.

This is a city built on ice... and pain. It was originally a gulag, so it's perfectly reasonable to assume that the frozen ground, dreary buildings, and rusty factories are now sitting on is a hybrid of hostile Siberian ice and hopeless political prisoners' tears. Between 1935 and 1956, 16,806 prisoners are known to have died in the harsh prison camp environment, either from the extreme weather conditions, starvation, or simply by being worked 'til they dropped. The sneaky Soviet Union continued to force more prisoners into the mines around the city all the way up to 1979.

Mining is still an important part of life in Norilsk as it is situated on one of the world's largest nickel reserves. There are also pockets of copper, cobalt, platinum, and palladium, as well as many coal seams which are still mined today. Extracting these raw materials and processing them at one of the city's many refineries has had a devastating effect on the environment, however. Dead trees, petrified and poking through the hard ground are common place, and there is little or no wildlife in the surrounding area. As a result, the people of Norilsk officially live in one of the 10 most polluted cities in the world, and regularly contend with dense smog and acid rain. Scientists estimate that 1 per cent of the entire planet's sulphur dioxide emissions come from just this town.

Since 2001, Norilsk has been "closed" to foreigners, apart from those from Belarus. It's a shame, as this means both the most northern mosque on Earth and the USSR's ballistic missile depot in the nearby Putoran Mountains aren't given their chance to shine as tourist destinations. Should you ever manage to sneak in and send a postcard home, however, you're bound to mention the weather. The city is blanketed in snow for between 250–270 days a year, with snow storms raging for up to three months at a time. Its Arctic location also means that during the winter the

sun doesn't rise for six weeks and locals endure temperatures up to -72 degrees Fahrenheit in total darkness. If you're desperate for a holiday glow, then go in July when there is constant sunshine for weeks on end and a minimum temperature of 25 degrees.

REBIRTH ISLAND, RUSSIA

Rebirth Island is not a chapter in a self-help book; it is a very real and very frightening place. It was once almost a paradise, with apricot trees, watermelon groves, and shoals of fish swimming gleefully off its sandy shores—but after four decades of playing host to the Soviet Union's top secret Microbiological Warfare Group lab, it is now nothing but an arid wasteland.

When traveling abroad, it's not uncommon to fall victim to new germs your body might never have encountered before. But no amount of vaccinations would save you on a trip to Rebirth, or Vozrozhdeniye Island as it's officially known.

The island is located in the Aral Sea, which was once the fourth largest inland body of water before the Soviet government started siphoning it off in the 1960s to irrigate nearby desert areas that were being used to grow cotton.

Vozrozhdeniye's position was deemed a great place to test out biological weapons, as the scientists decided there would be no chance of the bubonic plague, anthrax, and rabbit fever spores reaching neighboring Uzbekistan and Kazakhstan with all that water in the way. But soon nearly all the water was gone, transforming the island into a peninsula. The once isolated bio-weapon playground was suddenly not so safe.

As the Soviet Union crumbled, so too did the scientists' funding. They buried what was left of their germ stores all over the island, as well as more anthrax brought in from secret USSR strongholds. The entire process was done in such a hurry that some of the containers are feared to have leaked, releasing their deadly contents into the ground. It's not the local people who are most concerned by the toxic dump, however, but the US government. After the September 11 attacks, they spent US $6 million trying to decontaminate "Anthrax Island" so that no terrorists could go digging for free ammo.

ENERHODAR, UKRAINE

Located on the banks of the Dnieper River, the city of Enerhodar was originally built to house the workers of the nearby Zaporizhzhia Nuclear Power Plant. It is here that a fifth of all Ukraine's power is produced. It also holds the unenviable title of being the largest nuclear power station in Europe.

Today Enerhodar is home to almost 55,000 people, and not all of them are power plant employees. The city was founded in the early 1970s, and its name roughly translates

as "power gift." It depicts itself as a fantastic place, with local tourist agencies proudly declaring that "walking in such close proximity to one of the largest nuclear power plants in the world is a rare opportunity!"

But what is there to see other than a mass of thick concrete? How about the plant's 1,050-foot-high flue gas stack, which is Ukraine's highest freestanding structure. See it belch thick white clouds into the sky! See electricity pylons of 6,500 feet in height protrude from the river, dispatching clean nuclear energy to homes across the land!

The city sees itself as a cradle of culture. Every two years it hosts the international Good Theater Festival, which is always highly anticipated by the locals. It also boasts a well-stocked library—definitely one attraction not to miss.

And if you're a power plant fanatic looking for a comfortable night's sleep, you can even check yourself in to the city's Nuclear Power Station Hotel.

PRIPYAT AMUSEMENT PARK, UKRAINE

The children of Pripyat would no doubt have been delighted when they heard that a theme park was being built in their hometown. You can imagine them walking past the site each day on their way home from school, watching as metal structures sprouted from the ground and slowly began to form attractions such as a swing ride, a ferris wheel, and bumper cars, the freshly painted metal gleaming in the clear Ukranian skies.

The park was due to open on May 1, 1986 but, sadly, that day never came for Pripyat.

On April 26, just six days before its grand opening, one of the reactors at the nearby Chernobyl nuclear power plant exploded. The next day, Pripyat, a city of 49,000 that had been built to house the workers of the plant, was swiftly evacuated.

The residents never returned to the gray Soviet sprawl, which was just over one mile away from the doomed plant. The city remains just as it was left, right in the heart of the roughly 200 square mile Zone of Alienation, which is now only visited by avid urban explorers and a handful of morbid tourists.

Scientists studying the after-effects that the disaster had on the area have discovered that the radiation levels in the amusement park are among the highest in the city, and pictures taken in the park show that it is slowly being reclaimed by grass and trees.

The only ride still standing is the bright yellow ferris wheel, which remains in near-pristine condition and has become a haunting symbol of the city and the aftermath of its abandonment. Disneyland it certainly ain't.

MINSK, BELARUS

For thousands of girls in the ex-Soviet country of Belarus, selling their hair is the easiest way to make a living. It's a scenario that verges on Dickensian—girls sign contracts with "hair factories" that wait for their hair to grow to a certain length, before cutting it off and selling it to wig makers and Western countries as hair extensions.

The industry is particularly rife on the outskirts of the capital, Minsk, where poverty levels are higher and there are more girls desperate to support themselves and their families. Some "workers" even receive free meals while they grow their locks to ensure it's as strong and healthy as possible, while others are forced to cover their heads to protect the hair from pollutants that could

affect the value of the final crop. When the hair has reached the required length, the girls line up outside the factories ready to have their heads shaved before starting the process all over again.

Hair extensions used to be the realm of A-list superstars and glamour models, but these days it's becoming more common for women from all walks of life to have them, meaning demand for raw hair is higher than ever. Sadly, this doesn't mean that the donors receive a fair payment, with some girls receiving as little as US $30 for a handful of hair that would cost a wealthy woman $3,000 to have sewn, glued, or pinned in to her own hair at a glamorous salon in Paris, London, or New York.

Minsk: Wish you were hair?

BUGARACH, FRANCE

Bugarach is a tiny village at the bottom of Pic de Bugarach, the highest peak of the mountainous Corbières region in France. It offers spectacular views of the nearby Pyrenees and is popular with hikers and wine-lovers who come to sample some of the local vino.

But most visitors are there because they believe that Bugarach is situated at the base of an "alien garage."

For years, the Pic de Bugarach has been the focus of UFO fanatics and new-age hippies who think that it is holding several alien craft which will leave Earth for distant planets when the apocalypse comes. And as December 21, 2012 edges ever closer, so the number of visitors to this small hamlet increase. The town's population—which numbers less than 200—is so worried about a giant influx of hippies and new-age travelers that the mayor has requested the army's presence when December comes.

It all began when a local man claimed to hear humming from below the mountain and then happened to see a few aliens loitering around. His "report" was published in a UFO journal 10 years ago, and since then the town has been heralded as one of the few places that won't be destroyed when the end of days come.

The author of the report has (conveniently) died, but his legacy lives on in the form of spiritual healing centers, people hugging the mountain, and spontaneous meditation in the streets. The locals are enraged, and no doubt spooked, by the figures dressed in white robes who meet secretly in the woods after nightfall.

It can't be denied that Pic de Bugarach is a geological oddity, though. The top half of it is millions of years older than the lower half, which is made of limestone and lined with a series of caves. Its mysticism is said to have caught the attention of the Nazis and the Israeli intelligence agency Mossad, who both undertook archaeological digs on it. Rumors abound that it contains the Holy Grail, inspired Jules Verne's Journey to the Center of the Earth, and was a favorite place of the prophet Nostradamus.

DALBY, ISLE OF MAN

The Isle of Man's symbol is three legs joined at the thigh. If you think that's as weird as things get on this small island in the Irish Channel, then think again—it's also where the Manx cat originates, a breed of feline that has a stump instead of a tail.

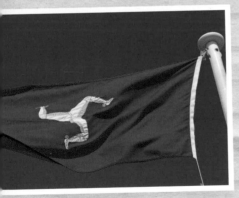

For years the island has been swathed in rumor and folklore. Locals tell of fairies that live under Ballona Bridge and demand to be noticed every June 20, of "merchildren" that were washed up on rocks in 1810, and the "wife seeker," a handsome male water spirit who every now and then kidnaps a human to be his bride. The Isle of Man also boasts its very own demonic beasts: the Bugganes, which are ogres covered in thick black hair and with huge talons. They look a lot like giant moles and sometimes talk to people. One is even said

to have ripped the roof off St. Trinian's church as the sound of its bells ringing woke it up.

But none of these tales compares to that of Gef, a talking mongoose who terrorized a family in the 1930s. The story gained such notoriety that journalists, spiritualists, paranormal investigators, and sightseers all flocked to Doarlish Cashen, a small, lonely farm on the outskirts of Dalby.

James Irving recalled that he first spotted the yellow-colored weasel in his farmyard, noting that the creature didn't spook his chickens. Later, it could be heard in the walls of the house, growling, spitting, and generally making a nuisance of itself. It learnt how to mimic animal noises and soon began reciting nursery rhymes. It didn't take long for the unwanted visitor to have full conversations with the Irving family, who claimed it had a clear voice, a few octaves higher than a human's. When they asked the creature who he was, he replied: "I am the ghost of a weasel, and I will haunt you with weird noises and clanking chains." He also told them his name was Geoff, spelt G-E-F.

Sometimes the entity would spook the family and their guests, throwing things and hurling abuse, while other times he would behave more benevolently and they would feed him bits of sausage and banana. Later, stories emerged of Gef hitching rides on buses, with one angry driver even claiming that Gef stole his sandwiches. Isle of Man: Weird.

PLUCKLEY, ENGLAND

Fancy a chinwag with the Devil? Then head to Pluckley in Kent. This quaint village, set in some of England's finest countryside, is said to be home to a bush that will summon the demon from the fiery depths of Hell if you dance around it 13 times.

And that's not all. The nearby Screaming Woods echo with the catcalls of souls who became lost in the dense forest and never found their way home. It's little wonder, then,

that Pluckley was named in the Guinness Book of Records as the "most haunted village in Britain," with 12 different ghosts reported.

The manifestations vary—a woman who committed suicide by eating poisonous berries can be heard calling for her hounds; a dead highwayman can be seen pinned to a phantom tree by gleaming swords at Fright Corner; the hanging body of a headmaster

is said to appear on Dicky Buss's Lane; home-owners report poltergeist activities; and blood-curdling shrieks have been known to ring out across the village during the night. A local taxi driver even claims to have picked up a passenger that simply disappeared minutes later.

But of all the village's spooky stories, none are as eerie as that of Lady Dering. It is said that she was buried in seven lead coffins which were then placed within another one made of oak in an attempt to prevent her body decaying. Many believe it is her spirit that causes the flickering of light in the Church of St. Nicholas in the dead of night, and she who causes the knocking sounds that come from beneath the floor. Outside the same church, a red lady stalks the graveyard, searching for her missing baby who was stillborn and buried in an unmarked grave.

MANCHESTER, ENGLAND

Statistics show Manchester's population is lacking in elderly people. Is this because of the 85,000 students who have come to study at one of the city's four universities? Or because the local OAPs have upped sticks to spend their twilight years sailing the high seas on a Saga cruise? To coin a Mancunian phrase, "is it 'eck!"

Put bluntly, if you live in Manchester your chances of living to a ripe old age are pretty slim. Lifestyle factors, such as heavy drinking, smoking, and a poor diet, are blamed for lowering the average life expectancy of the city's women to 79, a full decade less than females elsewhere in the country.

Manchester's reputation as a dangerous city is not to be ignored, either. Cases of burglary and car theft are commonplace, and Manchester also boasts its very own criminal underworld. Caution must be taken in areas like Moss Side and Longsight as there are gangs of teens who aren't afraid to shoot each other—or anyone else for that matter. These locals, or "scallies" are easily spotted throughout the region—just look for a scrawny youth with his tracksuit trousers tucked into his sports socks.

Thankfully, there's plenty to keep residents occupied before they meet their untimely (or indeed grisly) end. The huge student population love to party, making Manchester a binge-drinking hub. With bars and clubs at every turn offering rock-bottom drink prices, it's not unusual for the pavements to be awash with vomit, remnants of kebabs, and paralytic young people every Friday and Saturday night—and most weeknights, too.

Sometimes, the streets double up as arenas, with men and women goading each other to fight. Other times, it's the most romantic place on Earth, as couples stagger to the bus stop together, neither of them thinking that in a few hours they could be a part of Manchester's sky-high STD statistic.

Cheap booze also attracts hen and stag parties who, let's be honest, have the ability to make any town look messy. Similarly, legions of tramps enjoy hanging out in Piccadilly Gardens, ready to pester people for change as soon as they're off the tram. Be prepared to be called every name under the sun if you don't help them get their hands on extra-strength beer.

Oh, and to make matters even worse, it's also one of the rainiest places in the UK.

EGREMONT CRAB FAIR, ENGLAND

There are some people out there who think contorting their face as if it were made of dough is both big and clever. These are the kind of people you would find at the World Gurning Championships, which are held every September at the Egremont Crab Fair in Cumbria.

Gurning is the art of making the most horrible face you can, and is one of England's more unusual traditions. Men and women from across the country take place in regional heats, thus ensuring that only the best of the best make it all the way to Egremont.

One of the simplest—and most effective—gurns is sticking your chin forward, hiding your top lip with your lower one, puffing out your cheeks, and then crossing your eyes. People dedicate years to perfecting their gurns, and some even have their teeth removed to give their mouth more reach.

Some of the best gurners are the elderly, their gummy mouths and loose jowls allowing them to sometimes cover their noses with their lower jaws, and their misty, yellowing eyes giving them an extra unattractive edge. It's traditional for gurners to stick their head through a horse's collar when showing off their best grimaces, which is known as "gurnin' through a braffin'."

No one is sure when the contest began, or indeed why. And the competition isn't without its fair share of controversy—one year a man was disqualified for putting vinegar in his mouth to make his facial contortion even more pinched and uncomfortable to look at.

Other exciting events at Egremont Crab Fair include a pipe-smoking race and greasy pole climbing competition, where people try to shimmy up a lard-covered pole to retrieve a prize from the top.

ROODHARIGENDAG, BREDA, THE NETHERLANDS

Redheads like to moan that hating them is the last accepted form of racism, but, really, who can take them seriously with such ridiculous hair?

Sanctuary is at hand, however, in the Dutch city of Breda, which once a year hosts Roodharigendag, or Redhead Day. Around 5,000 (natural) redheads from across the globe meet in the central square at midday before taking to the streets, walking proudly with their heads held high—and without hats, hoods, or scarves to conceal their crowning glory.

The redheads are invited to take part in 50 different activities, ranging from the glamorous—artistic photoshoots, special flame-haired fashion shows, and dance routines by ginger beauties wielding barbecues and bananas on forks—to the intellectual, such as professors delivering lectures about hair, debates on history's greatest carrot-tops, and art exhibitions dedicated to the color red. It's mostly a social occasion, however, with the gingers being able to network and befriend others of their kind while various bands and musicians help to create an informal, joyous atmosphere.

The celebration gives men, women, and children whose hair represents the broad spectrum between subtle strawberry blonde and bright copper the opportunity to explore Breda without worrying about being heckled, teased, or stared at. But for anyone with an irrational fear of redheads, the old saying "one man's dream is another man's nightmare" is never more true than at Roodharigen.

LEKEITIO, SPAIN

Animal lovers be warned, a trip to the Basque fishing port of Lekeitio during the first week of September is definitely one to avoid. Every year, young men flock to the town to take part in Antzar Eguna, or "Day of the Geese," which is the pinnacle of the San Antolín festival.

A goose slathered in grease is suspended from a rope across the harbor. Then, as a test of his machismo and agility, a young man is rowed out into the bay, where he leaps up and grabs the goose's neck. Crowds of onlookers cheer and clap as the rope is pulled taut and then slackened, rapidly dunking the plucky lad and the goose in and out of the water.

As if holding on to the goose's greasy corpse wasn't hard enough, the aim is to rip or pull the head off the bird as quickly as possible. If you're successful, not only do you

get to keep the goose, but if you do it in the fastest time you will be declared the overall winner. If the competition ends in a tiebreak, a rather less grisly race around the harbor in row boats is used to decide the champion.

The festival of San Antolín, Lekeitio's patron saint, is 350 years old. Such competitions used to be the norm throughout Spain, but as time has gone on these old traditions have been gradually abandoned. It's certainly not an event for the squeamish, but at least these days the poor geese are dead; until recently, they would have been ripped apart while they were still alive.

KAVOS, GREECE

One week in Kavos will show you firsthand why British holiday makers are regarded as the scourge of Europe.

Up until the 20th century, the beautiful island of Corfu was popular with European dignitaries. Soaked in history and sunshine, it was an idyllic location for those with an interest in culture and a desire to tantalize their palate. Today it's a top island destinations for 80,000 young people who sign up for a week of hedonism with holiday provider Club 18-30. A lot of these youths have a very sure idea of what they'd like from their holiday: cheap booze, lots of casual sex, and English food—i.e. "none of that foreign muck." That's why the paradise setting of Corfu is so popular with these discerning travellers—its main town, Kavos, ticks all the right boxes.

Kavos offers the "most intense" nightlife on the entire island, which is predominantly found in a strip running through the center of town. Here, young people gather to enjoy the cheap alcohol deals, lining the streets shouting at each other, often having a quick scrap—or shag—down an alleyway.

A popular way to start a night out is by taking a straw and hunching over a fishbowl brimming with a sickly sweet cocktail, supping as much lurid alcohol as you can stomach—literally. By the end of the night the strip is awash with vomit, fast-food wrappers, and used condoms.

For bleary eyed colts with hearts set on a holiday romance, or perhaps just a badly coordinated fumble, there are many nightclubs for them to prowl around, playing tinny dance music until the break of day. Clubs also offer regular foam parties, where people find themselves up to their noses in acrid soapsuds. These should be seen as something of a double-edged sword—while they leave clothes stinking of upholstery cleaner and allow sexual predators to grope their way around the venue without being caught, they also provide vital assistance in helping ugly people score.

During the day, people hang around their budget hotel pools or head to the beaches to top up their tans, which turn from golden to copper as sunburnt Brits slather on tanning oil and roast themselves in the Mediterranean sun.

The result of all this is that Kavos is a no-go area for families, anyone over the age of 25, culture vultures, and teetotallers.

TYRNAVOS, GREECE

If you've ever wandered through a pleasant Greek town and thought, "Hmm, I wish I could drink from a cup shaped like a cock right now," then you're in luck.

Every year the streets of Tyrnavos are packed out with locals and tourists celebrating the ancient fertility festival of Bourani. Taking part on the first Monday of Lent—or

"Clean Monday" as it's also known—the festival is one of Greece's oldest traditions, and honors the god Dionysus, the town's patron saint. He's also the patron saint of wine and festivities, giving people the impetus to go extra mental—after all, it's what he would have wanted.

The locals parade through the streets while the bourani, a thick spinach soup, is cooked in giant pots in the main square. One of the key ingredients of the soup is

nettles, which are meant to give it an aphrodisiac quality. Apparently, they cause a sexy tingling in the genitals when it's time to urinate later on.

Chefs grab passers-by and make them lean over the vats of hot soup and give them a stir. Before they are let go, they have to sip some tsipoura, a raki-like beverage, from a cup shaped like a penis and kiss a ceramic phallus. Once they have done this, ash is put on their face.

The festival is all about penises, with knobs of all shapes and sizes being paraded through the streets, while male dancers grind the ground with their crotch while singing dirty ditties. Lewd jokes fill the air, and people sip drinks through drinking straws with a penis-shaped spout. Surprisingly, many families attend the event, and it isn't uncommon to see children carrying an effigy of an enormous todger, or cheering as their mother sips from a cock-shaped cup.

SONKAJÄRVI, FINLAND

From over the threshold to home from the pub after one bottle of wine too many, most men have had to carry their wives at some point. In Finland, wife carrying is a spectator sport, with the town of Sonkajärvi hosting an annual competition dedicated to it.

The first Wife Carrying Championship was held in 1992, and has steadily grown into an international event. Entrants come from as far afield as Australia and America to take part, while Estonia (which has a big wife carrying culture) also send their best "athletes."

Wife carrying is an important part of Finnish culture. In the late 1800s, men wanting to become troops had to prove they had the agility to steal a woman from a neighboring village, which was very common back then. These days the women participate willingly.

Two couples race the 253 meter track at the same time, running as fast as possible across sand, asphalt, and grass. There are also two obstacles, and an additional one-meter-

deep water section.
The women have to
wear a helmet, as it's
not uncommon for them
to be dropped. If this
happens, they have
to be picked up as
soon as possible before
completing the course.

There are also group
and team competitions.
The Group Wife
Carrying involves a
number of men
carrying one woman,
while the team event is more like a relay with men having to
drink a special "wife carrying drink" (beer) as the next
person begins. One of the most popular carrying styles is
the "Estonian method," in which the woman has her face in
the small of the man's back, gripping his waist with her
arms and wrapping her feet around his neck.

Teams don't actually have to be married, and any pair can
participate as long as the woman is over 17 and weighs at
least 108 pounds, or 49 kilos. While it might seem like a
good idea to get the lightest partner you can find, when
you consider that the prize for first place is the woman's
weight in beer it should come as little surprise that most
men start thinking that bigger is most definitely better.

INDEX

INDEX

ACKNOWLEDGMENTS